HOW DO I BECOME A . . . ?

VETERINARIAN

Mindi Rose Englart

Photographs by Melanie Stengel

BLACKBIRCH®
PRESS

THOMSON
★
GALE

San Diego • Detroit • New York • San Francisco • Cleveland • New Haven, Conn. • Waterville, Maine • London • Munich

For more information, contact
The Gale Group, Inc.
27500 Drake Rd.
Farmington Hills, MI 48331-3535
Or you can visit our Internet site at http://www.gale.com

Photo Credits: All photos © Melanie Stengel, page 7 © Andrew Cunningham

LIBRARY OF CONGRESS CATALOGING-IN-PUBLICATION DATA

Englart, Mindi.
   A veterinarian / by Mindi Rose Englart.
      p. cm. — (How do I become a: series)
Includes index.
Contents: Kinds of veterinary medicine — The study of disease — Licensing and further education — Preparing for surgery.
   ISBN 1-56711-750-3 (hardback : alk. paper)
   1. Veterinarians—Juvenile literature. 2. Veterinary medicine—Vocational guidance—Juvenile literature. [1. Veterinarians. 2. Veterinary medicine—Vocational guidance. 3. Vocational guidance.] I. Title. II. Series.
   SF756.E54 2004
   636.089'069—dc21   2002013544

Printed in China
10 9 8 7 6 5 4 3 2 1

CONTENTS

Dedication
To my cousins Michael, Stephanie, Hilary, Shayna, Noah, Amy, and Sandy (and their animals)

Special Thanks
The publisher and the author would like to thank Barbara R. Donato and Rebecca Russo and the Tufts University School of Veterinary Medicine in North Grafton, Massachusetts, as well as Susan Landon and Dr. Morgan MacKay at the New Haven Central Hospital for Veterinary Medicine in New Haven, Connecticut. The author would also like to thank editors Claire Kreger and Janet Reed Blake. If you would like more information about the university or animal hospital featured in this book, visit www.tufts.edu/vet or www.centralpetvet.com.

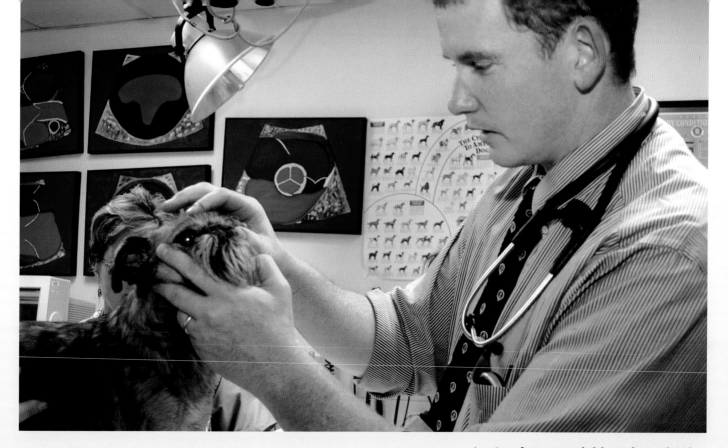

Veterinarians care for the health of all kinds of animals. These animal doctors treat
pets, farm animals, and even wild animals. There are about 60,000 veterinarians in
the United States today. Most veterinarians work in clinics, where they treat sick or
injured animals and help owners keep their animals well. Others work at research
laboratories or zoos. It takes a lot of work to become a veterinarian. It also takes
a special love for animals. So, how does someone become a veterinarian?

Even the largest zoo animals need ▲
veterinarians to keep them healthy.

Kinds of Veterinary Medicine

More than half of all veterinarians (vets) treat companion animals. Those are animals that people keep as pets. These vets care for the health of dogs, cats, birds, hamsters, reptiles, rabbits, and other animals.

Some veterinarians work with farm animals, such as horses, cows, and pigs. These doctors often drive to farms or ranches to see their patients. They teach farmers and ranch owners how to properly feed and house their animals. They also treat wounds, set broken bones, perform surgery, and give medicine to prevent diseases. They even help animals give birth. Large-animal veterinarians often work outdoors, in all kinds of weather.

Other veterinarians care for zoo, aquarium, or laboratory animals. Some veterinarians work in public health and research. They study animal diseases, and diseases that both people and animals can get. For example, research veterinarians discovered that Lyme disease can infect many different animals. This disease also affects humans.

Animals with jobs—such as police dogs—need good care to perform well.

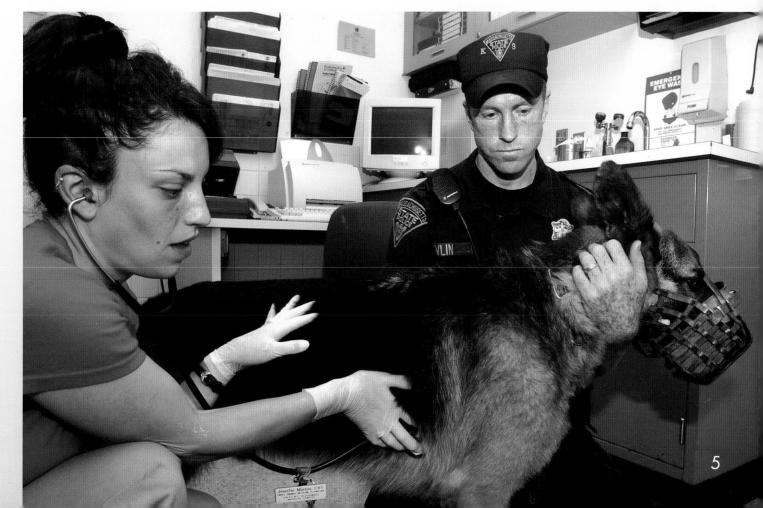

Veterinary students have done well in ▲
biology and zoology in college.

Applying to Veterinary Medical School

Getting into a veterinary medical school can be very hard. There are only 28 veterinary schools in the United States, and there are lots of people who want to become veterinarians.

To prepare for veterinary school, a person must go to college and get good grades in classes such as biology (the study of living things), zoology (the study of animals), chemistry, and English. To get into most veterinary schools, a person must take a test, such as the Graduate Record Examination or the Veterinary College Admission Test.

In addition to college classes, a person must have experience working with animals. Working on a farm or at an animal shelter is a good way to get this experience.

In the Classroom

Tufts University School of Veterinary Medicine is in North Grafton, Massachusetts. It takes 80 new students into its veterinary medical program each year. New students learn how healthy animals behave. They take courses in biochemistry (the chemical processes in living things) and physiology (how organs work). They also take classes in anatomy (how bodies work). They learn about how different animals breed.

In some classes, students practice solving medical problems. For example, a teacher might say that an animal is drinking a lot and seems tired. Students will work alone or in groups to figure out what is wrong. To solve medical problems, students need to study. They also write papers about what they have learned. They must learn to think like veterinarians.

▲ Many veterinary schools have a
farm where students can practice
caring for large animals.

On the Farm

Tufts veterinary students spend lots of time with animals. The campus has a farm where students can practice giving physical exams to sheep or cows. They learn about proper nutrition for different animals. They learn to keep horses, goats, and pigs healthy. They also learn to treat farm animals that become sick or injured.

At Tufts, students take care of
▼ sheep and other animals.

Keep Your Pets Safe

Many people do not know that common household items can poison a pet. Some of them are not harmful to people, but can hurt or kill an animal. Here are some things to keep away from pets:

- Chocolate
- Salt
- Onions
- Tomato leaves and stems
- Moldy foods
- Mothballs
- Batteries
- Modeling clay
- Cigarettes

Students study the relationship between animals and humans in veterinary school.

Ethics

Some veterinary schools teach ethics—how to answer difficult questions when right and wrong answers are not clear. In these classes, students learn about animal-human relationships and try to answer hard questions. For example, they talk about when it is okay to test new medicines on animals. They also talk about ways to prevent pet overpopulation and animal abuse.

Years of School

During the first year of veterinary school, students learn what makes animals healthy. They learn what healthy organs and bones look like and how they function. In their second year of school, students learn about diseases animals can get. Animals and people can get many of the same diseases and conditions —such as cancer, diabetes, and skin problems. Some diseases, such as heartworm, are unique to animals. Cats and dogs can get this life-threatening disease from mosquito bites.

Students use a microscope ▶ to study an animal tissue sample.

11

Veterinarians must also work well with the owners of animals. In the third year of school, students learn this skill. At the end of the third year, students spend time with experienced veterinarians. Together, they see patients at an animal hospital. During this time, students may watch or help doctors. Some students also work outside the school, at a zoo or a research lab. The third year of veterinary school is the last year of classes.

Students watch and help veterinary doctors as part of their training.
▼

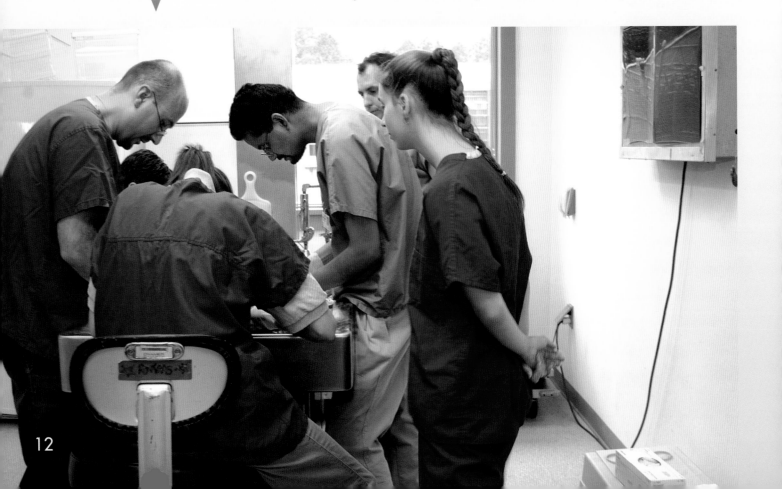

▲ **Samples from sick animals that died are studied by veterinary students.**

Fourth-year students treat patients. At the Tufts veterinary hospitals, students take care of large and small animals. Experienced veterinarians watch students carefully and help them. Fourth-year students study animals that have died to learn more about diseases that harm and kill. To do this, they take tiny samples of diseased skin or muscle or bone and look at them under a microscope. They look for clues that may show a disease, such as cancer or a virus.

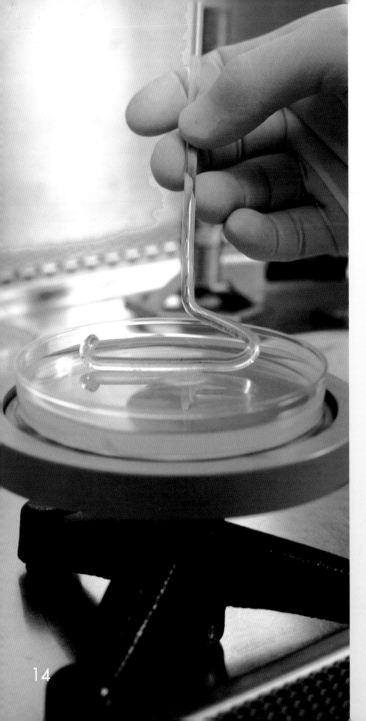

Lab Classes

In lab classes, students do lots of scientific experiments. They use microscopes to look at things that are too small for the eye to see. They study healthy cells and diseased cells. They learn what different types of bacteria (germs that can make an animal sick) look like. Students also learn from books, models, and films.

In some labs, veterinary students grow bacteria to study them. Some bacteria grow so fast they can double their number in 20 minutes. Students study bacteria such as E. coli that cause diseases. This bacteria can grow in meat from cows. It can cause food poisoning in humans. As they discover how and why these bacteria cause diseases, veterinarians can also work to prevent them.

◄ **Studying bacteria in a lab is a useful way to learn about diseases.**

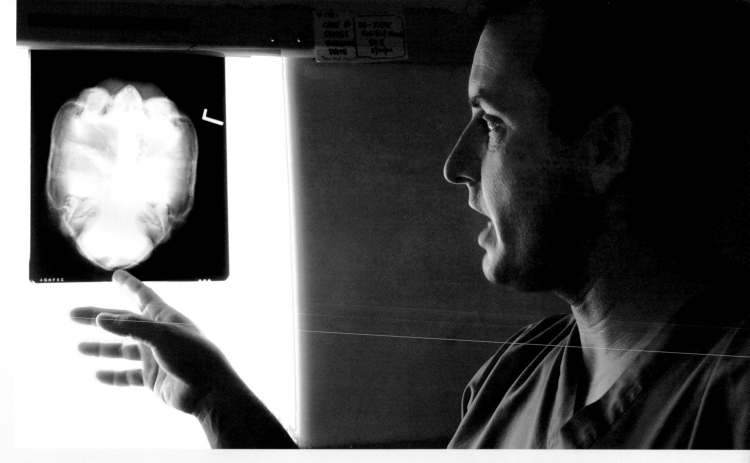

Seeing Patients

Students learn to diagnose and treat problems in animals. There are many ways to diagnose a patient. For example, Xrays can show that a bone is broken. Blood tests can tell if an animal has an infection or other disease. Students learn all about medicines and how to give the right ones to each patient. They learn the math needed to figure out the right doses for different kinds and sizes of animals. They also learn how to keep accurate medical records.

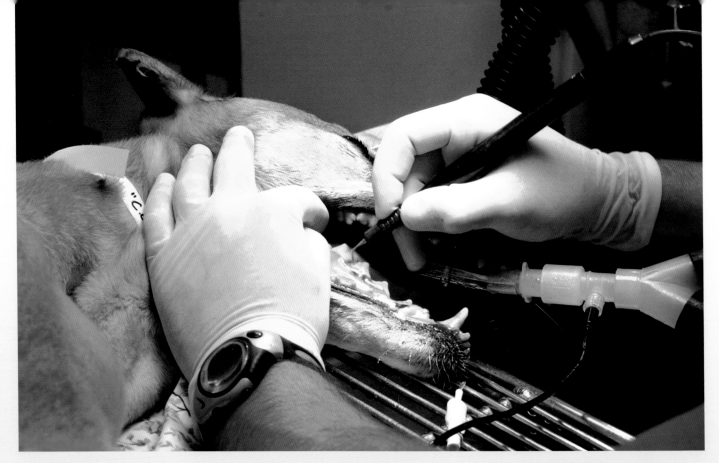

Learning Animal Dentistry

Animals need to have their teeth cleaned, just like people. But a veterinarian can't tell a dog to open its mouth and relax. Veterinary students learn to give animals a drug to make them fall asleep for a short time. This can be dangerous if the animal is not healthy. Students learn how to test an animal's heart, liver, and kidneys before giving it any drugs. While the animal sleeps, the student learns to clean the teeth and to fill cavities without pain to the animal.

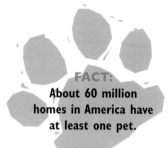

FACT:
About 60 million homes in America have at least one pet.

At Work in the Animal Hospital

An animal hospital is a lot like a human hospital. There are lots of emergencies in both places. Like human doctors, veterinarians need to be able to make important decisions quickly.

Veterinary students hang photos of their pets in their classrooms. ▶

17

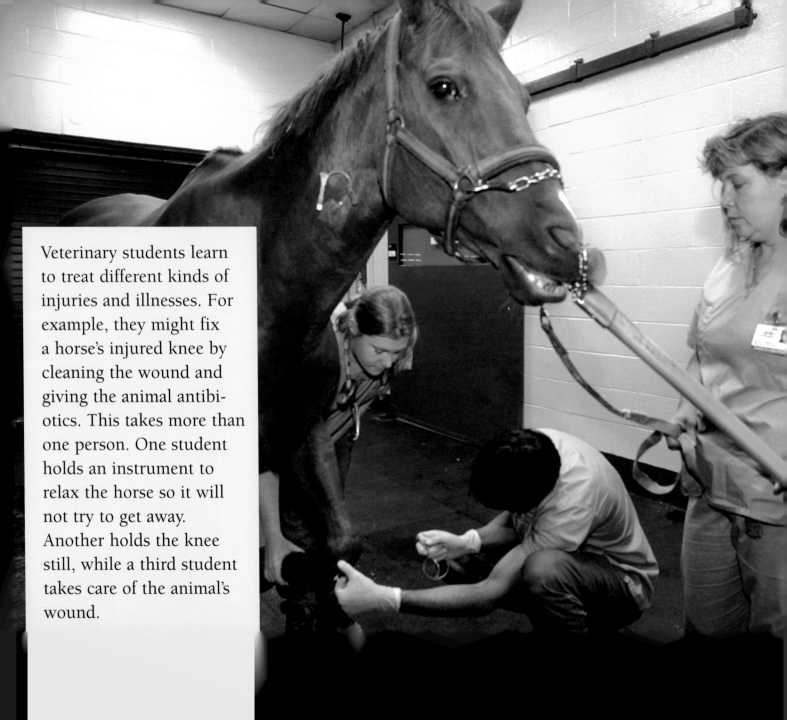

Veterinary students learn to treat different kinds of injuries and illnesses. For example, they might fix a horse's injured knee by cleaning the wound and giving the animal antibiotics. This takes more than one person. One student holds an instrument to relax the horse so it will not try to get away. Another holds the knee still, while a third student takes care of the animal's wound.

Students learn how to remove tumors (lumps that may be diseased) from all kinds of animals—even from goldfish! Vets in training learn to give medicine by putting a small amount in the fish's water. If a fish needs an operation, it is removed from its tank. The student pumps water over the fish's gills so it can breathe during the surgery. After surgery, the student gives the fish a dose of antibiotics to help prevent infection.

A veterinarian shows a student how to examine a goldfish for a tumor. ▶

◀ **It takes at least three people to treat a horse's knee.**

19

Wildlife Clinic

At Tufts' Wildlife Clinic, students treat injured turtles, owls, birds, deer, and other wild animals. Veterinary students must be careful when handling any animal. They must be especially careful with wildlife, though, because they are not used to people. If an animal is afraid, it may scratch or bite. Wild animals may also carry diseases. For this reason, students wear thick gloves to protect their hands from getting scratched.

A barred owl gets ▶ physical therapy.

A turtle with ▼ a wired shell.

Wild animals need the same help that other animals do. They need physical therapy when their muscles or bones are injured. They may need surgery, or antibiotics, or stitches if they have been hit by a car or in a fight with another animal. Students learn how important it is to not try to tame (make pets of) wild animals. This way, when the animals are well again, they can go back to living in the wild.

WARNING: Never touch an injured animal. Always get an adult to help you take the animal to a clinic for care.

Licensing and Further Education

After students have finished four years of veterinary school, they must pass a test before they can practice veterinary medicine. This test, called the North American Veterinary Licensing Exam (NAVLE), is given on a computer. It takes a day to complete and has 360 multiple-choice questions about all parts of veterinary medicine.

Some students want further training after they graduate. These students may complete a one-year internship (on-the-job-training) after veterinary school. Those who want to focus on one type of veterinary medicine—for example, surgery—take an additional three-year program called a residency. There are over 20 areas a veterinarian can specialize in, including the brain, the skin, or the heart.

◀ **Some students decide to specialize in the treatment of certain kinds of animals, such as exotic birds.**

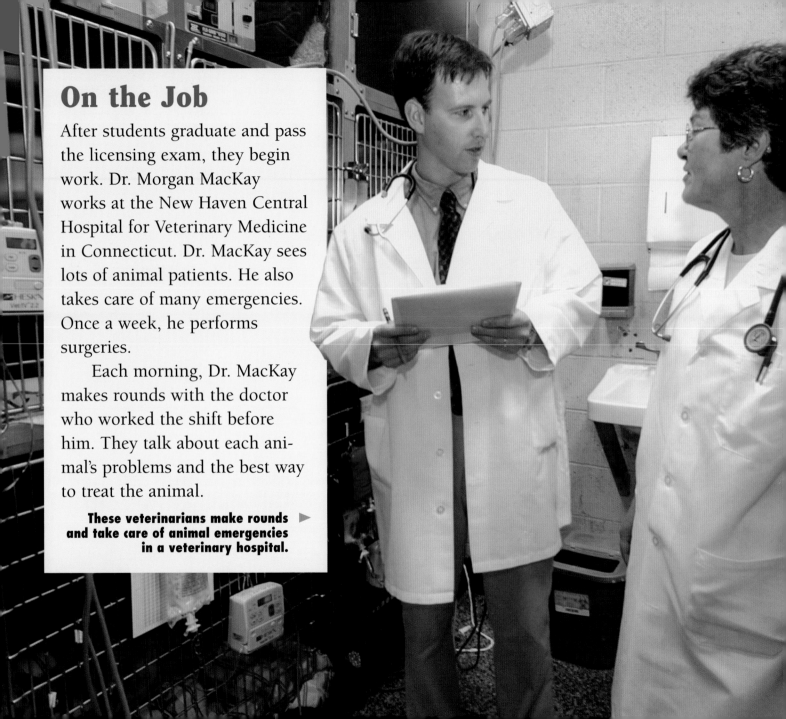

On the Job

After students graduate and pass the licensing exam, they begin work. Dr. Morgan MacKay works at the New Haven Central Hospital for Veterinary Medicine in Connecticut. Dr. MacKay sees lots of animal patients. He also takes care of many emergencies. Once a week, he performs surgeries.

Each morning, Dr. MacKay makes rounds with the doctor who worked the shift before him. They talk about each animal's problems and the best way to treat the animal.

These veterinarians make rounds and take care of animal emergencies in a veterinary hospital. ▶

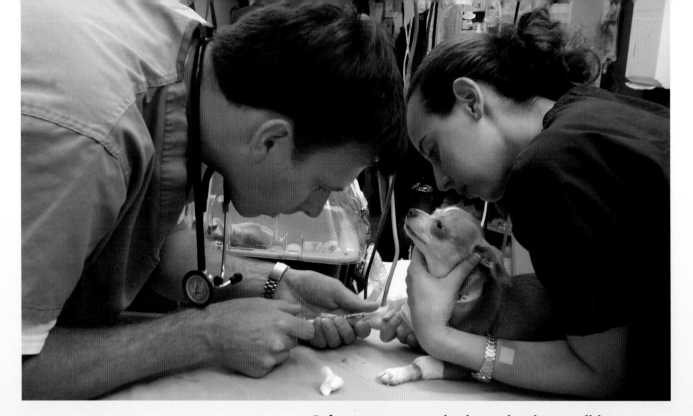

Surgery

Veterinarians perform all types of surgery. The most common surgery is called spaying (for females) or neutering (for males). This surgery is done on pets, such as cats and dogs. During this type of surgery, a veterinarian removes the reproductive organs of an animal. Spaying or neutering keeps pets from having unwanted babies. This is important because there are hundreds of thousands more pets than there are homes for them. These unwanted animals must try to survive on their own without shelter, food, or medical attention. Often, they suffer. They may also carry diseases that could make other animals and humans sick.

Before surgery, an animal is given medicine so it will not feel any pain. Then the area where the surgery will take place is shaved and cleaned. Next, the veterinarian washes his or her hands thoroughly and puts on sterilized (germ free) clothes. During surgery, special machines monitor an animal's heart and other body functions. These machines will alert the veterinarian if there is a problem during surgery. The veterinarian uses a sharp knife to make a small cut in the animal. After surgery, the veterinarian uses special thread to close the cut with sutures (also called stitches).

▼ **Shaving the animal's fur before surgery.**

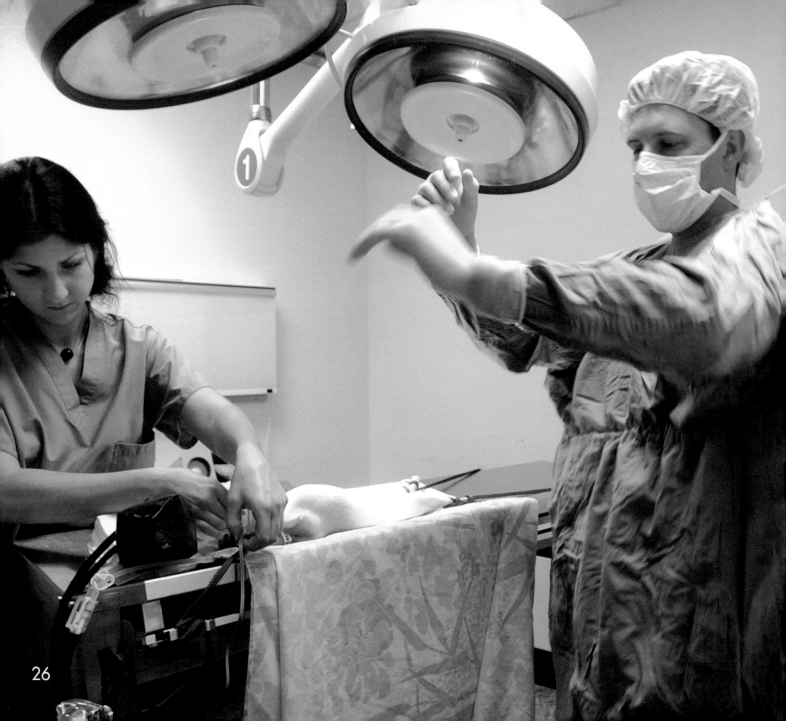

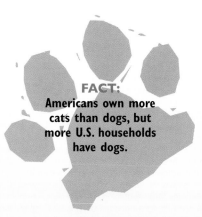

After surgery, the veterinarian speaks with the animal's owner. The veterinarian tells the owner how to make the animal comfortable while it recovers. The vet also tells the owner how long it will be before the animal is healed.

◀ **In the operating room.**

Euthanasia

Euthanasia is when doctors humanely help to end the life of a suffering patient. Sometimes, an animal is so sick or in so much pain it cannot get well. Then the veterinarian and the animal's owner must make a difficult decision: do they let the animal live in pain or do they perform euthanasia to stop its suffering? This is one of the hardest parts of a veterinarian's job. If the decision is to perform euthanasia, the veterinarian gives the animal medicine that will end its life painlessly. This is also known as "putting an animal to sleep."

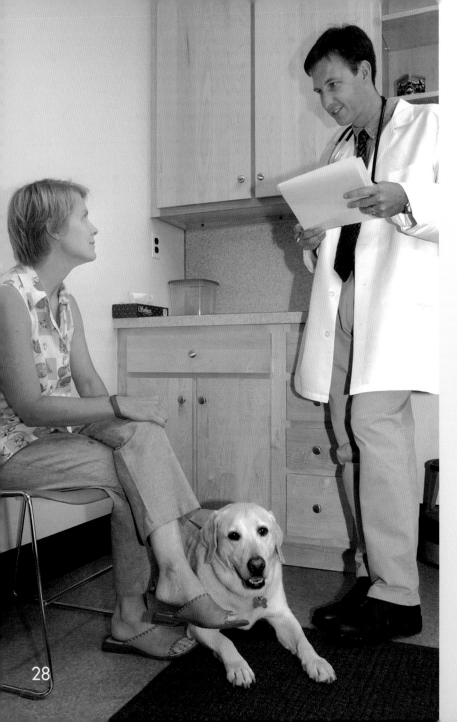

Wellness Exam

Animals get checkups just like people do. A veterinarian starts by looking at the patient's chart, which is a record of earlier visits. The chart has lots of information about the animal's health. The veterinarian asks the owner about the animal's behavior. Have there been any changes in its eating or drinking? Has the animal been peeing more or less than usual? Does the animal seem to be unusually tired? The veterinarian also makes sure the animal receives medicine that helps to prevent diseases such as rabies

Next, the veterinarian examines, or looks at, the animal. He or she checks its ears. The

◄ **Veterinarians ask pet owners lots of questions.**

veterinarian may lightly rub a swab (a small stick with cotton on the end) in an ear to get a sample for the lab if there seems to be a problem. This sample can be tested for infection, ear mites, or allergies. The veterinarian also weighs the animal. He or she will use a stethoscope to listen to the animal's heart.

A veterinarian must update charts after every office visit. The information on a patient's chart helps the veterinarian keep track of the animal's medical history. The veterinarian also spends quite a bit of time on the phone. Between patient visits, he or she calls animal owners to give lab test results and to answer any questions they have about their pets.

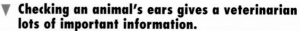

▼ **Checking an animal's ears gives a veterinarian lots of important information.**

29

It is important for owners ▲
and vets to share information
about an animal.

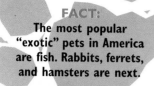

Until Next Time

Over time, a veterinarian develops a relationship with a pet and its owner. The veterinarian and the owner are able to work together to spot health problems before they become serious.

At the end of an office visit, the veterinarian takes a few minutes to talk with the owner and to answer any last questions. Then he or she says goodbye till next time!

Saying goodbye. ▶

Glossary

Antibiotics Medicines that fight infections

Bacteria Germs that can make an animal sick

Biology The study of living things

Ethics How to answer questions when right and wrong answersare not clear

Euthanasia Painless procedure to end an animal's life to stop it from suffering

Spay Surgery to remove the reproductive organs from female animals

Neuter Surgery to remove the reproductive organs from male animals

Zoology The study of animals

For More Information

Books

Bownam-Kruhm, Man. *A Day in the life of a Veterinarian.* Rosen Publishing Group, 1999.

Marino, *Betsy. Emergency Vets.* Discovery Kids, 2001.

Websites

Tufts School of Veterinary Medicine
www.tufts.edu/vet

Index